Fifteen Iraqi Poets

NEW DIRECTIONS POETRY PAMPHLETS

#1 Susan Howe: *Sorting Facts; or, Nineteen Ways of Looking at Marker*

#2 Lydia Davis / Eliot Weinberger: *Two American Scenes*

#3 Bernadette Mayer: *The Helens of Troy, NY*

#4 Sylvia Legris: *Pneumatic Antiphonal*

#5 Nathaniel Tarn: *The Beautiful Contradictions*

#6 Alejandra Pizarnik: *A Musical Hell*

#7 H.D.: *Vale Ave*

#8 Forrest Gander: *Eiko & Koma*

#9 Lawrence Ferlinghetti: *Blasts Cries Laughter*

#10 Osama Alomar: *Fullblood Arabian*

#11 Oliverio Girondo: *Poems to Read on a Streetcar*

#12 *Fifteen Iraqi Poets* (ed., Dunya Mikhail)

Fifteen Iraqi Poets

Edited by Dunya Mikhail

New Directions Poetry Pamphlet #12

The Poetry Foundation / Harriet Monroe Poetry Institute / Poets in the World series

Cover design by Office of Paul Sahre
Interior design by Eileen Baumgartner and Erik Rieselbach
Manufactured in the United States of America
New Directions Books are printed on acid-free paper.
First published as New Directions Poetry Pamphlet #12 in 2013

Library of Congress Cataloging-in-Publication Data
Fifteen Iraqi poets / edited by Dunya Mikhail.
pages cm.—(New Directions poetry pamphlet ; #12)
ISBN 978-0-8112-2179-5 (alk. paper)
1. Arabic poetry—Iraq—Translations into English. 2. Arabic poetry—20th century—Translations into English. 3. Arabic poetry—21st century—Translations into English. I. Mikha'il, Dunya, 1965– editor of compilation.
PJ8044.5.E5F44 2013
892.7'160809567—dc23   2013030598

POETRY

FOUNDATION

Fifteen Iraqi Poets is a copublication of the Poetry Foundation and New Directions Publishing Corp. This book is published as part of the *Poets in the World* series created by the Poetry Foundation's Harriet Monroe Poetry Institute.

"The Poetry Foundation" and the Pegasus logo are registered trademarks of The Poetry Foundation. For more information about The Poetry Foundation, please visit www.poetryfoundation.org.

10 9 8 7 6 5 4 3 2 1

New Directions Books are published for James Laughlin
by New Directions Publishing Corporation
80 Eighth Avenue, New York, NY 10011

CONTENTS

Preface   7

1. Badr Shakir al-Sayyab
   Rain Song   11

2. Nazik al-Malaika
   New Year   18

3. Abdul Wahab al-Bayati
   From the Papers of Aisha   22

4. Mahmoud al-Braikan
   On Freedom   25

5. Yousif al-Sa'igh
   Dinner   27

6. Sargon Boulus
   Elegy for Sindibad Cinema   30

7. Saadi Yousef
   Cavafy's Residence   34

8. Fadhil al-Azzawi
   Spare Time   37

9. Sherko Bekas
   Separation   41

10. Hasab al-Sheikh Ja'afar
    God's Palm Tree   43

11. Ronny Someck
    Jasmine: Poem on Sandpaper   47

12. Taleb Abd al-Aziz
    My Brother's War   49

13. Ra'ad Abdul Qadir
    His Life   53

14. Abdulzahra Zeki
    The Guard   55

15. Siham Jabbar
    Like Hypatia in Ancient Times   57

Acknowledgments   61

PREFACE

As I was putting together this mini-anthology, I learned something very exciting about the history of Iraqi poetry. But before I share my little discovery, I want to emphasize that what I learned relates not only to these fifteen poems but to the many other poems I read in making this slim selection. It was a nearly impossible task trying to pick only fifteen grains of sand from a shimmering desert. There is a saying in my country that if you throw a stone in Iraq, it will likely fall onto the head of a poet! In his poem "Nothing but Iraq," Mahmoud Darwish writes, "For poetry is always being born in Iraq, so become Iraqi to become a poet, my friend." Beginning in the 1940s, when the free-verse movement started in my homeland and gradually spread to other Arab countries, a major topic of discussion in the Arab literary world has been the "legality" or "illegality" of breaking the rules of classical poetry known as *a'muudi*. The metrical rules of *a'muudi* were set by Al-Khalil ibn Ahmad al-Farahidi in the eighth century. Al-Farahidi established sixteen meters of verse for poets to follow, each rhythmic pattern—called *bahr* or "sea"—included a hemistich in each line as well as end rhymes. Today, the free verse of Arabic poetry still makes use of rhyme, while the poetic line is open to more rhythmic flexibility without the hemistich and varies in length. The prose poem in Arabic has completely broken with classical forms. Writers of prose poetry have defended their work against accusations that "this is not poetry," saying their poems contain a more organic "inner rhythm."

What I discovered as I read more and more poems is that modern Iraqi poetry is a natural continuation of Sumerian poetry, and that classical *a'muudi* verse is in fact a tradition that branched from the river of Iraqi poetry. The words from Sumer in southern Iraq were our first cries of poetry, etched in a cuneiform script onto clay tablets, the lines unfolding in one long prose poem without rhymes but with an "inner rhythm." The texts are shaped by a narrative, but the repetition of lines and the intensity of images are unmistakably lyrical. Most of the narratives are broken into fragments, though it is often impossible to discern if the fragmentation is intentional or due to missing or crumbling tablets. Sumerian poetry is inherently metaphorical, its metaphors naturally surfacing from primitive images and symbols used to convey complex ideas. The language lost some of its original metaphorical vividness as it evolved into Akkadian and other Semitic equivalents. In modern times the rediscovery of the writings of Sumer only dates back to the mid-nineteenth century.

Features of Sumerian poetry reappear in the DNA of modern and contemporary Iraqi poetry. Its myths and symbols apparent in the writings of the pioneering poets Badr Shakir al-Sayyab and Abdul Wahab al-Bayati, and these codes became indicators of modernity. Living in a state of continuous wars and massacres, Iraqi poets have often lamented the destruction of their country with a common opening plea: "O Iraq." This longing directed to ruined cities was very common in Sumerian poetry. For instance, such pleas in one text titled "Lamentation on the Destruction of Ur" is directed sometimes to the place without naming it ("O my city," "O my house") and other times to named cities ("O Nippur," "O Isin," "O Eridu," "O Uruk"). The "Lamentation" consists of eleven songs totaling 436 lines, the fifth and sixth songs describing the destruction of Ur as a "devastating storm." Delving into our recent collective memory, one recalls that the First Gulf War was code-named Operation Desert Storm by the U.S. government. Both usages of "storm" were figurative as war was the real cause of destruction in both cases. The eleventh song is a prayer to Nanna to restore the Sumerian people to their homeland, Ur.

To feel threatened by the new forms of modern poetry was easier than bringing the dead back to life. The oral culture of Arab society contributed to the popularity of *a'muudi* poetry, which spread through recitation (*ilqa'*) rather than through reading. Many of the poets were illiterate and the strict meters carried their verses along. Some *a'muudi* lyrics are filled with playful rhythms and powerful images that, when chanted or sung, make listeners' heads sway with the feeling of *tarab* ("pleasing to the ear"). The phenomenal singer Um Kalthoum popularized many of these tunes, as well as the poets of her generation who penned them. *A'muudi* poetry is also closer to the Quran musically, making it more familiar to Arab ears. The codes of the Sumerian poetic tradition were totally unfamiliar to modern-day Iraqis, even after they became readable. The pioneers and innovators of our new poetry were perhaps more influenced by the poetry of the Americas than by Sumerian poetry, but their fruits have the unmistakable taste of the Sumerian tree.

DUNYA MIKHAIL

I.

RAIN SONG

BADR SHAKIR AL-SAYYAB

Translated from the Arabic by Lena Jayyusi and Christopher Middleton

Your eyes are two palm tree forests in early light,
Or two balconies from which the moonlight recedes
When they smile, your eyes, the vines put forth their leaves,
And lights dance ... like moons in a river
Rippled by the blade of an oar at break of day;
As if stars were throbbing in the depths of them ...

And they drown in a mist of sorrow translucent
Like the sea stroked by the hand of nightfall;
The warmth of winter is in it, the shudder of autumn,
And death and birth, darkness and light;
A sobbing flares up to tremble in my soul
And a savage elation embracing the sky,
Frenzy of a child frightened by the moon.

It is as if archways of mist drank the clouds
And drop by drop dissolved in the rain ...
As if children snickered in the vineyard bowers,
The song of the rain
Rippled the silence of birds in the trees ...
Drop, drop, the rain ...
Drip ...
Drop ... the rain ...

Evening yawned, from low clouds
Heavy tears are streaming still.
It is as if a child before sleep were rambling on
About his mother (a year ago he went to wake her, did not
    find her,
Then was told, for he kept on asking,
"After tomorrow, she'll come back again ...")
That she must come back again,
Yet his playmates whisper that she is there
In the hillside, sleeping her death for ever,
Eating the earth around her, drinking the rain;
As if a forlorn fisherman gathering nets
Cursed the waters and fate
And scattered a song at moonset,
Drip, drop, the rain ...
Drip, drop, the rain ...

Do you know what sorrow the rain can inspire?
Do you know how gutters weep when it pours down?
Do you know how lost a solitary person feels in the rain?
Endless, like spilt blood, like hungry people, like love,
Like children, like the dead, endless the rain.
Your two eyes take me wandering with the rain,
Lightnings from across the Gulf sweep the shores of Iraq
With stars and shells,
As if a dawn were about to break from them,
But night pulls over them a coverlet of blood.
I cry out to the Gulf: "O Gulf,
Giver of pearls, shells and death!"
And the echo replies,

Feelings of loneliness

12

As if lamenting:
"O Gulf,
Giver of shells and death ..."

I can almost hear Iraq husbanding the thunder,
Storing lightning in the mountains and plains,
So that if the seal were broken by men
The winds would leave in the valley not a trace of Thamud.
I can almost hear the palmtrees drinking the rain,
Hear the villages moaning and emigrants
With oar and sail fighting the Gulf
Winds of storm and thunder, singing
"Rain ... rain ...
Drip, drop, the rain ..."

And there is hunger in Iraq,
The harvest time scatters the grain in it,
That crows and locusts may gobble their fill,
Granaries and stones grind on and on,
Mills turn in the fields, with the men turning ...
Drip, drop, the rain ...
Drip ...   *never ending*
Drop ...

When came the night for leaving, how many tears we shed,
We made the rain a pretext, not wishing to be blamed
Drip, drop, the rain ...
Drip, drop, the rain ...
Since we had been children, the sky
Would be clouded in wintertime,
And down would pour the rain,

And every year when earth turned green the hunger struck us.
Not a year has passed without hunger in Iraq.
Rain ...
Drip, drop, the rain ...
Drip, drop ...

In every drop of rain
A red or yellow color buds from the seeds of flowers,
Every tear wept by the hungry and naked people,
Every spilt drop of slaves' blood,
Is a smile aimed at a new dawn,
A nipple turning rosy in an infant's lips,
In the young world of tomorrow, bringer of life.
Drip, drop, the rain ...
Drip ...
Drop ... the rain...
[Iraq will blossom one day in the rain.]

I cry out to the Gulf: "O Gulf,
Giver of pearls, shells and death!"
The echo replies
As if lamenting:
"O Gulf,
Giver of shells and death."
And across the sands from among its lavish gifts
The Gulf scatters fuming froth and shells
And the skeletons of miserable drowned emigrants
Who drank death forever
From the depths of the Gulf, from the ground of its silence,
And in Iraq a thousand serpents drink the nectar
From a flower the Euphrates has nourished with dew.

*people trying
to escape*

I hear the echo
Ringing in the Gulf:
"Rain ...
Drip, drop, the rain ...
Drip, drop."
In every drop of rain
A red or yellow color buds from the seeds of flowers.
Every tear wept by the hungry and naked people
And every spilt drop of slaves' blood
Is a smile aimed at a new dawn,
A nipple turning rosy in an infant's lips
In the young world of tomorrow, bringer of life.

And still the rain pours down.

·

Badr Shakir al-Sayyab (1926–1964) was born in the small town of Jaykour, south of Basra. His father was a date farmer, and his mother died giving birth to her fourth child when he was six. In the 1940s, influenced by the modernist movements in Europe and the United States, al-Sayyab and Nazik al-Malaika launched a free-verse movement, consciously rupturing the strict forms of classical Arabic poetry while turning to more personal themes and imagery. Al-Sayyab's first collection of poems, *Azhar Dhabila* (Withered Flowers), published in 1948, still followed the classical rules of prosody. At the time he was teaching English at a secondary school, and a year later he was imprisoned for his activities with the Communist Party. When he was released, he was banned from teaching for ten years. After working many odd jobs, including a position as a date taste-tester, he moved to Kuwait in the early 1950s. During this time his second book appeared, *Asaatiir* (Legends), which not only fully embraced the free-verse style but was concerned with fresh, new themes, turning to historical legends, such as the pre-Islamic tribe of Thamud, who were said to have been wiped out by an earthquake that was brought about by infidelity. He also transformed his own surroundings and memories, like the small river Boayb in his hometown, into a personal mythology. Gradually he shifted from a traditional romanticism to more political and social themes.

In 1960, al-Sayyab's book *Inshodat al-Mattar* (Rain Song), which included his popular poem of the same title, was published—a significant event in the world of modern Arabic poetry. The repetition of "rain" in the poem initially evokes a sense of sadness, but by the end it has changed to joy, the tone of the poem seamlessly shifting from pessimism to optimism. Al-Sayyab's romantic language flows with a harmony that develops as if it had already existed, like the drops of rain from an unquestionable source. For much of his life, al-Sayyab suffered from poverty and illness. After living in Basra for some time he moved back to Kuwait and died there at age thirty-eight from a degenerative nerve disorder. Al-Sayyab published seven poetry collections, in addition to translations of Louis Aragon, Nâzım Hikmet, and T. S. Eliot.

2.

NEW YEAR

NAZIK AL-MALAIKA

Translated from the Arabic by Rebecca Carol Johnson

New Year, don't come to our homes, for we are wanderers
from a ghost world, denied by man.
Night flees from us, fate has deserted us.
We live as wandering spirits
with no memory
no dreams, no longings, no hopes.
The horizons of our eyes have grown ashen
the gray of a still lake,
like our silent brows,
pulseless, heatless,
denuded of poetry.
We live not knowing life.

New Year, move on. There is the path
to lead your footsteps.
Ours are veins of hard reed,
and we know nothing of sadness.
We wish to be dead, and are refused by the graves.
We wish to write history by the years.
If only we knew what it is to be bound to a place;
if only snow could bring us winter
to wrap our faces in darkness.

If only memory, or hope, or regret
could one day block our country from its path.
If only we feared madness.
If only our lives could be disturbed by travel
or shock,
or the sadness of an impossible love.
[If only we could die like other people.)

The anger of living a dull life

•

During times of war and crisis, people die together in groups rather than individually. They die young or in the middle of their lives and not necessarily old and in bed. The last line of "New Year" expresses this truth perfectly. To understand the importance of Nazik al-Malaika (1923–2007), one must consider the essentially patriarchal rhetoric of Arabic poetry that she wrote against. To break the strict conventions of the classical tradition was an enormous achievement. Al-Malaika is acknowledged not only for changing the course of Arabic poetry but also for writing pioneering works of criticism, such as her essay "On Contemporary Poetry," thus paving the way for future poets. She was an incisively intelligent woman who was deeply engaged with the social issues of her times. In 1953, al-Malaika delivered a lecture at the Women's Union Club titled "Women Between Two Poles: Negativity and Morals," calling for women's rights in Arab society. She actively spoke out against honor killings, where the murder of a woman by male family members for actions that bring "dishonor" to the family—such as having an affair before marriage, or refusing to enter an arranged marriage—is protected by the law. Al-Malaika also formed an organization for women who opposed marriage, offering a safe haven to those who did not choose to embrace the wife's traditional role.

Al-Malaika, one of seven children, was born in Baghdad. Both of her parents were poets, and by the age of ten she was writing verse in classical forms. As a child she also learned to play the oud (a stringed instrument akin to the lute) and took acting classes. She studied Arabic at the Baghdad Teachers Training College and English at the British Council, and continued her studies at Princeton University and at the University of Wisconsin, where she earned a master's degree in comparative literature. She then returned to Iraq, married a fellow student in the Arabic language department, and with her husband helped found the University of Basra. They had one son together. For many years al-Malaika taught at the University of Kuwait but was forced to return to Iraq in 1990. When the Gulf War ended a year later, she moved to Cairo with her family. There she died at age eighty-three, after struggling with Parkinson's for many years, leaving behind several books of poetry, essays, and a memoir.

3.

FROM THE PAPERS OF AISHA

ABDUL WAHAB AL-BAYATI

Translated from the Arabic by Bassam K. Frangieh

She said: "I will kill him
and carry his head to my tribe,
an idol to worship
to burn when they fight.
In the desert
I build a temple for love.
In his name
the birds seek refuge.
In a time of hunger
I wear tatters
and slaughter my camel.
At the door of his temple I lament."
She said: "I will carry him
a ring on my finger.
As the ages pass
I'll weep and mourn in his grave."

•

In 1995, when I was living in Amman, Jordan, I used to frequent the café at the Feneq Gallery, a lively meeting place for literary and cultural events. The café was special not only because of its vibrant atmosphere and excellent coffee but because Abdul Wahab al Bayati (1926–1999), one of Iraq's free-verse pioneers, was often there, presiding at what was commonly known as "al-Bayati's table," surrounded by young poets. White hair, a gentle smile, gray suit and tie: this is how I remember al-Bayati. Once, when he was asked why he chose to settle in Jordan after wandering half the globe, al-Bayati replied that he was tired of exile and so he chose the city nearest his birthplace, Baghdad. Al-Bayati lived most of his life outside Iraq, and frequently switched residences and jobs. In Iraq, he was an editor for the magazine *Al-Thaqafa al-Jadida* (New Culture), which was shut down by the monarchy government for its leftist views, and al-Bayati was jailed for several months. After his release, he moved from Syria to Lebanon, and then to Egypt, teaching temporarily at various universities. He also worked as a cultural attaché in Moscow where he met the Turkish poet Nâzım Hikmet. His friendship with Hikmet inspired his poetry collection *A Letter to Nâzım Hikmet and Other Poems* (1956). After the 1958 revolution that brought an end to the monarchy, al-Bayati returned to Baghdad where he worked as the director of the translation and research department at the Ministry of Education. Some years later, he resumed his position as a cultural attaché, this time in Madrid. During the 1990s he moved between several Arab cities, and died at age seventy-three in Damascus. Al-Bayati was the author of twenty books of poetry, including *Love, Death, and Exile* (2004), translated by Bassam K. Frangieh.

In Arabic, *aisha* means "alive." Al-Bayati has used this word as a proper name in many of his poems since his collection *Al-Mawt Fi al-Hayat* (Death in Life, 1968). In poems such as "Aisha's Orchard," "Aisha's Profile," "Elegy at Aisha's Grave," among others, Aisha is depicted as a dead woman, a woman who has returned from the dead, a spirit of a blue butterfly, a daughter of a legendary king, a killer, a lover, or a bride sleeping in a grave. Is Aisha a personal myth imagined by al-Bayati, or was she a real person al-Bayati had known since his childhood? A neighbor? First love? Or perhaps a symbol for the feminine and poetry as she is in his poem "Shiraz's Moon": "I see all women of the world in the one who is born from my poetry." I asked the translator, Bassam Frangieh, if Aisha was dead in the poems, and he replied, "Aisha is never dead. She is his hope, his hero, his lover, his savior, who is eternally alive."

4.

ON FREEDOM

MAHMOUD AL-BRAIKAN

Translated from the Arabic by Haider al-Kabi and Rebecca Carol Johnson

You called on me to discover
another continent,
but denied me a map.
I'd rather sail in my little boat
so that if we should meet
it will be worth remembering.

You offered me a house
furnished and comfortable
in exchange for a song
that meets your demands.
I'd rather stay on my swift horse
and roam
from one gust of wind
to another.

You brought me a new face
beautiful, perfectly proportioned.
I thank you
but I'd rather not have a glass eye
or a plastic mouth.
I have no desire to rid my face of its difference,
nor do I care much for symmetry.
I thank you
but let that distinction remain.
[At heart is the slave master not also a slave?]

•

Everything about Mahmoud al-Braikan (1931–2002) inspired curiosity: his poetry, his life, his death. He used to hide his poems in a safe so that others couldn't publish them. The few poems that circulated among his peers were enough to elevate him into the ranks of modern innovators. He rarely spoke in public or gave interviews. "A poet dies twice: Once when he is published, and once when a statue is erected in his name," al-Braikan said in a speech about Badr Shakir al-Sayyab. (A statue of al-Sayyab was constructed in 1972 at the Basra Corniche.) He chose a life of isolation during the Gulf Wars when many writers were in the business of "battle mobilization." His distance from literary and social activities, and his silence, was interpreted by some as an uncompromising stance against dictatorship, by others as passive disengagement. In the end, his silence might not have been golden, but his poetry will always be a rare, precious stone.

"On Freedom" was written under the watchful eye of the Iraqi dictatorship. In exchange for propagandistic support, the government frequently offered a house and other privileges to well-known poets, though it was unclear what this support implied and to accept it meant to blindly follow the government's directives. To preserve one's freedom and individuality could come at a high cost, and yet in this poem al-Braikan playfully affirms this freedom to choose.

Al-Braikan studied law at the University of Baghdad, though he never did anything with this degree. Instead, he taught Arabic language and literature at the Teachers Training College in Basra until he retired in the 1990s. He was also an accomplished calligrapher and judged many poetry contests for Basra secondary schools. On February 28, 2002, al-Braikan was killed in his home in Basra, apparently by thieves. He is buried near his friend, the poet Badr Shakir al-Sayyab.

5.

DINNER

YOUSIF AL-SA'IGH

Translated from the Arabic by Saadi Simawe

Every evening when I come home
my sadness comes out of his room
wearing his winter overcoat
and follows me.
I walk, he walks with me
I sit, he sits next to me
I cry, he cries for me
until midnight
and we are tired.
That is when I see
my sadness enter the kitchen
open the refrigerator door
take out a piece of black meat
and prepare my dinner.

•

When Yousif al-Sa'igh (1933–2005) died at age seventy-two, a heated debate arose among Iraqi writers over whether to commemorate him or not. They were divided between those who opposed it because of his association with the Ba'ath Party and Saddam's regime, and those who wanted to honor him for his art. In the end, no official memorial was held, though most Iraqis would agree that al-Sa'igh is an important figure in modern Iraqi poetry.

Al-Sa'igh was born into a Christian family in Nineveh—his father was a priest and his uncle a bishop. He was an Arabic teacher in secondary schools before working as a journalist. During the 1980s, he was the general director of the Department of Cinema and Theater. Though al-Sa'igh was raised as a Christian, he later converted to Islam. He underwent another enormous ideological change as a Marxist and then became a committed Ba'athist. His poetry, however, wasn't evangelical or propagandistic. Sadness, love, and loss are common themes in al-Sa'igh's work, but what makes many of his poems particularly interesting is their portrayal of vulnerability and the unexpected relationships he draws through linguistic parallelism. His poetry mixes narrative and lyrical elements in quiet tones, and is ritualistic—a ritual in which the poet pretends not to take part but instead looks on curiously through the keyhole with his third eye, the poet's eye.

Al-Sa'igh's collection *Sayidat al-Tufahat al-Arba'* (The Lady of the Four Apples, 1971) was written after his first wife died in a car accident and the apples she had just bought rolled out from the wreckage. His book *I'tirafat Malik Bin al-Raib* (Confessions of Malik Bin al-Raib, 1972) is a poetic biography that caused a great stir due to its experimental style, its length determined by the time it took for a snakebite to kill the poet al-Raib. I recall one time al-Sa'igh canceled an official meeting in his office to attend a poetry reading that I had with other young poets. "Thank you for coming," I said to him. He smiled and handed me a drawing, saying it had been inspired by one of my poems I had read. Al-Sa'igh was a painter and a member of the Iraqi Artists Society.

6.

ELEGY FOR SINDIBAD CINEMA

SARGON BOULUS

Translated from the Arabic by Sinan Antoon

There is a road
adorned with ceilings
washed by memory
until they are white
under a sky at the apex of its agony
where I walk
where my words want to rise like the stairs of a castle
like sounds ascending the lost scale
one note after another
in my friend's notebook
the oud player who died of his own silence in the desolation
of exile
I find that sound
I find the building and open a door to it:
Our time, how it has lost its tickets!
It is flowing in the dark
like a tiny stream of voices
the voices of those who no longer have a voice
telling me
that they had demolished Sindibad Cinema
What a loss!
Who will sail now?

Who will meet the old man at sea?
They demolished those evenings:
our white shirts, Baghdad summers
Spartacus, The Hunchback of Notre Dame, Samson and Delilah
How will we dream of traveling now?
And to which island?
They demolished Sindibad Cinema
The drowned man's hair
is heavy with water
He had returned to the party
after they turned off the lights
piled the chairs on the barren riverbank
and chained the waves of the Tigris

•

Sargon Boulus (1944–2007) was born to Assyrian parents in al-Habbaniya, near a British military base and an artificial lake. When he was thirteen his family moved to the city of Kirkuk, by the al-Qa'em River. Many of his poems reflect a fascination with water that can be traced to his childhood in al-Habbaniya and Kirkuk. Politically, Kirkuk is an economically important city because of its rich oil deposits, while culturally, in the 1960s, it was rich with the poetry of the Kirkuk Group. Boulus was a member of this group, along with other prominent writers such as Fadhil al-Azzawi, Jan Demmo, Muayad al-Rawi, and Salah Faiq.

In 1966 Boulus moved to Lebanon after Yousef al-Khal, the publisher of the innovative literary magazine in Beirut, *Shi'r* (Poetry), published sixteen of his poems and asked him to work for the magazine. But with little money and no residency papers, Boulus was arrested and imprisoned a few years later. His literary friends convinced the Lebanese president and the U.S. ambassador of Boulus's importance and he was given an entry visa to the United States. He arrived in New York in 1969 and eventually made his way to San Francisco where he met many writers of the Beat generation and lived on a boat with hippies. He had already published an Arabic translation of Ho Chi Minh's poems titled *Yawmiyat Fi Sijn* (Prison Diary) when he witnessed the large opposition to the war in Vietnam on the streets of San Francisco. He describes this experience in his first book of poetry, *Al-Wusool Ila Madinat Ain* (Arrival in the City of Where, 1985). Boulus translated the sonnets of Shakespeare and poems by Ezra Pound, W. H. Auden, Shelley, Sylvia Plath, Allen Ginsberg, Robert Duncan, Pablo Neruda, and Rainer Maria Rilke, among others. Other books of poetry followed, as well as a collection of short stories and an autobiography.

"Elegy for Sindibad Cinema" is from *Azma Ukhra li-Kalb al-Qabila* (Another Bone for the Tribe's Dog, 2008). Before the 2003 invasion of Iraq, movie theaters in downtown Baghdad screened mostly Egyptian and Hindi films, and were often crowded with families on the weekend. Eventually religious groups closed most of the theaters and other places of entertainment. Boulus's poem is an elegy to all those "demolished" memories and dreams of traveling to other places seen in the films.

7.

CAVAFY'S RESIDENCE

SAADI YOUSEF

Translated from the Arabic by Ferial J. Ghazoul

10 rue Lepsius:
Is your Alexandria the sea?
Or is it the circularity
of the narrow alley where light disperses like boiled snails?
Perhaps your Alexandria
is the door
I cannot find.
Perhaps it is the mumblings
from these lips, so garbled
it cannot venture forth.
Perhaps it is the vase
or the palace balcony where the god
had forsaken Antony.

10 rue Lepsius:
From where do the nocturnal Greeks rise out?
From where does the wine flow out?
And the lilting song?
The shattered bouzouki?
The air that is alas alas alas . . .
The air that is an "ahh" in the abyss of "ahh" . . .

10 rue Lepsius:
The balcony darkens
The room retreats through the wardrobe's mirror
The shirt flutters toward the sea
The sea vanishes
....
If you are Antony, wait,
a god may rise from the broken
mirror and call your name ...

•

The Greek poet Constantine Cavafy had a profound influence on modern Arabic poetry, and on Saadi Yousef in particular, to the extent that Yousef has translated more than one hundred and twenty poems by Cavafy into Arabic. His poem "The God Abandons Antony" is set in Cavafy's birthplace, Alexandria, and Yousef alludes to the imagery of this poem in his own poetic address to Cavafy. For the last twenty-five years of his life, Cavafy lived at 10 rue Lepsius in Alexandria. Yousef wrote "Cavafy's Residence" after visiting the poet's home not long before it was transformed into a museum by the Greek consulate. He once said that he learned how to write poetry from reading Cavafy and imitating him.

Saadi Yousef was born in 1934 in Abu al-Khasib, a village south of Basra. He attended elementary school in the village, but as there was no secondary school he had to travel to Basra each day to attend classes. He went on to Baghdad University to study Arabic literature. Upon graduating, Yousef returned to Abu al-Khasib to work as a teacher in the newly opened secondary school. Three years later he visited Moscow and eventually returned to Baghdad as a devoted communist.

In Iraq, 1958 was a time of turmoil and change: the Hashemite monarchy was overthrown and the country became a republic. The era ended with the Ba'ath Party's rise to power. Yousef was among those who were imprisoned due to his affiliation with communism. He was released in 1964, and in the following years lived in several cities in the Middle East. He returned to Baghdad in 1972 and worked for the Ministry of Culture but was forced to leave again in 1978, this time for good. He continued his itinerant life in the Middle East, then lived in Africa and Europe, before settling in London in 2000. He is the author of several books of poetry and prose, including *Without an Alphabet, Without a Face: Selected Poems* (2002), translated by Khaled Mattawa, and *Nostalgia, My Enemy* (2012), translated by Sinan Antoon and Peter Money.

8.

SPARE TIME

FADHIL AL-AZZAWI

Translated from the Arabic by Khaled Mattawa

During long, boring hours of free time
I sit and play with a globe.
I form countries without police or prisons
and throw out others that lack consumer interest.
I make roaring rivers flow through barren deserts
and form continents and oceans
that I store away for the unknown future.
I draw a new colorful map of nations:
I roll Germany into the Pacific Ocean, teeming with whales,
and I let refugees sail
pirate ships to her coasts in the fog,
dreaming of the promised garden in Bavaria.
I switch England with Afghanistan
so the young Brits can smoke hashish for free
courtesy of Her Majesty's government.
I smuggle Kuwait from its fenced and mined borders
to the Comoros, the islands
of the moon in its eclipse,
keeping the oil fields intact, of course.
I move Baghdad
into the loud drumming
of Tahiti.
I let Saudi Arabia crouch in its eternal desert
to preserve the purity of her thoroughbred camels.
I accomplish all this before

surrendering America back to the Indians
just to give history
the justice it has lacked for so long.
I know changing the world isn't easy
but it's still necessary despite everything.

•

Fadhil al-Azzawi was born in 1940 in Kirkuk, where four languages are commonly spoken: Arabic, Turkish, Kurdish, and Assyrian. Like many other children, he was sent to the mullah before attending school, and at the mosque he learned to recite the Quran by heart. By the time he started school, he was memorizing classical poems and discovered the *One Thousand and One Nights*. Al-Azzawi once wrote to me: "I was swept away, not only by its magical world, but also by the eroticism of its language. In school during the day, I pretended to be an angel. The teachers upheld traditional moral values and it was impossible to talk about sex or use vulgar words and expressions. But at night, Scheherazade transformed me into a devil. She opened up all the closed doors for me and led me into the real daily lives of people, telling me about their dreams and fantasies." He called those days of childhood "a magical feast." At an early age he was also profoundly influenced by Will Durant's *The Story of Civilization*, saying that "it enabled me to see the huge efforts made by all generations and nations to make life on our planet possible and more humane."

One day during his childhood, al-Azzawi visited the American Cultural Center in Kirkuk to borrow books in English. They initially refused as one needed to be twelve to receive a library card. He challenged them, saying, "You can test me and see if I know English or not." They did and he passed. So he began reading Erskine Caldwell, William Saroyan, John Steinbeck, Robert Frost, and William Faulkner.

In the 1960s, al-Azzawi, along with Sargon Boulus, was active in the Kirkuk Group, a circle of young writers and poets who played a leading role in the renewal of Iraqi and Arabic literature. His mother, however, said to him, "Is it true, my son, that you are writing poetry and want to be a poet? Shame on you! We want you to be a respectable man, not a beggar and conjurer. You know the only business Arab poets can find today is writing poems in praise of rulers and chieftains for a handful of dinars. How could we face people if we had such a son?" Recalling this, al-Azzawi said to me, "What my mother said wasn't far from the truth. The poet's main business during *al-jahiliya* [the pre-Islamic era] was to defend the tribe through poetry and to praise the sheikhs. Most of the great Arab poet al-Mutanabbi's poems were written in praise of emirs and sultans." Al-Azzawi comforted his mother by telling her, "I know an English poet named T. S. Eliot who became the director of a bank in London." His mother replied, "Well then, it's all right to carry on with your poetry writing if you are going to be the director of a bank." At the age of eighteen, al-Azzawi left Kirkuk to study English literature at the University of Baghdad. He later earned a doctorate in cultural journalism from Leipzig University, and eventually settled in Berlin. Though he never became a banker, he has earned his living as a writer, translator, and journalist, and is the author of several books of poetry, fiction, and criticism, including the book of poems *Miracle Maker* (2003), translated by Khaled Mattawa, and three novels translated by William Maynard Hutchins: *The Last of the Angels* (2007), *Cell Block Five* (2008), and *The Traveler and the Innkeeper* (2011).

9.

SEPARATION

SHERKO BEKAS

Translated from the Kurdish by Reingard and Shirwan Mirza

If they deprive my poems
of flowers
one of my seasons will die.

If they deprive my poems
of my beloved
two of my seasons will die.

If they deprive my poems
of bread
three of my seasons will die.

If they deprive my poems
of freedom
my whole year will die
as will I.

•

Sherko Bekas was born in 1940 in Sulaimaniya, Kurdistan, in northeast Iraq. His father was the popular Kurdish poet Fayak Bekas. In 1965 Bekas joined the Kurdish freedom fighters and worked at the movement's radio station, the Voice of Kurdistan. Due to political pressure, he left Iraq in 1986 and settled in Sweden. The following year he received the Tucholsky Scholarship from the Swedish PEN Center. In 1991 he returned to Kurdistan to support the Kurdish National Uprising. Bekas was nominated as a member of parliament and served as the first minister of culture in Kurdistan, a position he held for a year before resigning. He has published more than thirty books, all in Kurdish, and most have been translated into Arabic. A three-volume edition of his poetry in Kurdish was published in Sweden in the 1990s. A pioneer of modern Kurdish poetry, Bekas is known for introducing a free-form style called *ruwanga* (vision) as well as the "poster poem" into Kurdish poetry—short, intense, often epigrammatic poems with an urgent tone, like warm sandwiches eaten on the go. Bekas lived in Sulaimaniya and was president of Sardam Publishing House.

The Kurds are known for their deep fondness for nature—their history and traditional Yazidi religion are rooted in the Zagros Mountains, the many caves of which they've escaped to during times of war. Bekas's poetry treats nature not simply as something beautiful but as context for philosophical thought. Readers can find a whole garden in a poem of his where the flowers, the trees, and the birds serve as an archival memory for the suffering of a nation. In his will, Bekas has asked to be buried in Azadi Park, Sulaimaniya's largest public park, "so that young lovers who visit the park can stop by my grave." Municipal officials, however, say this is not legal. While this pamphlet was being typeset, Bekas passed away on August 4, 2013.

10.

GOD'S PALM TREE

HASAB AL-SHEIKH JA'AFAR

Translated from the Arabic by Rebecca Carol Johnson and Dunya Mikhail

My old robe on you waves in the north
Christ-like, and the plain taste of your dates
taken by the ravens and the wind, heavy with dust,
scatter over it from sunrise to evening,
its shadow a banner of defeat.
Where are the children
climbing like birds to the sky?
Before our arms turned rigid, scorched by the midday heat
we would extend to you our little hands
in a plea for the world to rain gifts
and to taste, before the birds come, dates
shining like mirrors, upon the luxurious beds of grass
in your bright shade covered with morning dew.
O God's only palm tree in the wind,
every night you fill my long solitude with tears
so I rise, I come to you ... but I only embrace
the tall shade, I only touch the dust.
As alone as your trunk, a shadow burned by absence,
I dry out like a pale star or a twig.
"O palm tree in the wind," I used to say, "O my desiring heart,
after a year or more I will return to her with
my own stumbling steps, for everything I lost remains in her
hands.

If I return what would remain of you? In your body?"
The summer nights were heavy with singing
your heavy branches in the wind.
And I would appear with my eyes closed,
one of your buds a heaven of coiled leaves, shining in green.
I wake up in a rush before the birds, and in my hands
the water of the summer's night to pour upon you.
So if I come what would remain of you but ashes
in our deserted hut, and the soughing wind in the ravine
that sweeps my papers away. Was it all in vain my longing?
O palm tree in the wind, our eyes are strained with waiting,
we watch the days and count the ripened fruit
as the sun drops and the rain falls on you
the shining dates fill our little hands like candles.
So if I return what would remain of you? And what would
    remain of me?
The children grew up and so did the playful world, but I
used to say, "O palm tree in the wind: O my eager heart . . .
So if I return what would remain of you? What would
    remain in your body?"

•

Hasab al-Sheikh Ja'afar was born in Missan in 1942. He has published more than a dozen books of poetry and a memoir, *The Dervish's Ashes*. In 1959, Ja'afar won a scholarship to study in Moscow, and eventually graduated with a master's degree in literature from the Gorky Institute. In an interview some years later, Ja'afar says that when he was in Moscow he missed Iraq, and when he returned to Iraq he missed Moscow. He has translated many Russian poets into Arabic, including Anna Akhmatova, Pushkin, Alexander Blok, and Vladimir Mayakovsky. Ja'afar became known for his "circular poetry," where each sentence in a poem doesn't stop at the end of a poetic line, but runs over to the following line, or in some cases the poem consists of one sentence. This is far from unusual in American and European poetry but at the time it was quite rare in Arabic poetry. Though his early poems were written in the classical style, they were modern in spirit and content.

In 1983, Ja'afar won the Soviet Peace Award. In the mid-1990s, he lived with a friend in a tin shack in Amman, Jordan. Because of the political situation, he asked the UN office for asylum but his request was denied. He returned to Iraq when the Saddam regime was overthrown in 2003. A year earlier he had received the Al Owais Award for poetry from the government of the United Arab Emirates, a $100,000 prize that Saadi Yousef received in 2004, though it was later retracted after Yousef criticized the president of the UAE. The judge's citation for the award noted that Ja'afar possesses a "rare awareness that enabled him to contribute to the rise and enrichment of new Arabic poetry. He developed lyrical, dramatic, and narrative forms, drawing deeply from his culture's folk traditions. His poems are fresh and astonishing."

The palm tree in Ja'afar's poetry doesn't exist solely as an object of nature; it also serves as a collective symbol of childhood and homeland. Palm trees are everywhere in Iraq and the people have a profound emotional connection to them. This is evident in the language itself as Iraqis have hundreds of names for the fruit of the palm. *God's Palm Tree* is also the title of Ja'afar's first poetry book, published in 1969.

II.

JASMINE: POEM ON SANDPAPER

RONNY SOMECK

Translated from the Hebrew by Moshe Dor and Barbara Goldberg

Fairuz raises her lips
to the sky
so that it will rain jasmine
on those who've met only once
unaware they're in love.
At noon I am listening to her in Muhammad's Fiat
on Ibn Gabirol Street.
A Lebanese singer singing in an Italian car
owned by an Arab poet from Baqa al-Gharbiyye
on a street named for a Hebrew poet who lived in Spain.
And jasmine?
If it falls from the sky at the End of Days
it will be for a moment
a green
signal
at the next intersection.

•

Ronny Someck was born in Baghdad in 1951 and moved with his family to a transit camp near Tel Aviv as a young child. "I left with an empty box of memories," Someck has said, "but I have secondhand memories. My parents, my uncles, and grandparent, all talked about their homeland." Someck studied Hebrew literature and philosophy at Tel Aviv University and drawing at the Avni Academy of Art. He told me that he learned to write poetry by listening to the great Arab singers Umm Kulthum and Fairuz, as well as to Elvis Presley and Billie Holiday. "I wasn't aware of any differences between the two cultures," he said. Someck has published eleven volumes of poetry, including *The Fire Stays in Red* (2002), translated by Moshe Dor and Barbara Goldberg, as well as a children's book he wrote with his daughter. His poems have been translated into forty-one languages, and he has released three recordings with the musician Elliott Sharp. Someck currently teaches literature in a secondary school and runs writing workshops.

I asked Someck about the sandpaper in the title of his poem, and he replied, "Muhammad in this poem is my friend Muhammad Hamza Ganaim. Sandpaper is a metaphor for our friendship and our lives." For Someck, the poet who lives in Israel is like a pianist in an old American Western. "His piano sits in the corner of a saloon, a place that always smells like gunpowder. He knows the saloon is not a concert hall, and when he's threatened he can only reply, 'I have nothing to do with this situation. I am only the pianist.'"

12.

MY BROTHER'S WAR

TALEB ABD AL-AZIZ

Translated from the Arabic by Haider al-Kabi

Get up, brother, the war is over.
They have taken your tank to the smelter
but your rifle still lies on the mountain.
At last, the sand has erased your courage
and farmers plant fields where you fell.
The trees that you planted
have died. The enemy has taken the mountain
you vowed you would never abandon.
From its ice-covered summit
they've lowered your banner, which was raised
until your downfall.
They've plundered your uniform and your splendor
and no matter how dead you were
they kept riddling your corpse with their bullets.
Though worms crawled out of your eyes
and your large heart, they still couldn't
believe you were dead—
you had been their worst nightmare.
Get up, brother, the war is over.
The children have surrounded the garden.
The balls of flaming metal
have expired, and the children
now kick them around—
save the one ball that fell beside you

and tore your body apart.
We're back in the village now,
without wars and without enemies.
Horizons of dewy nightingales
surround our pillows.
Slowly, we're forgetting our old wounds,
and though our daggers bring back memories,
all we really want
is for our dogs not to bark at anyone
except our guests.
My mother is still in bed.
I spoke with her of your height and your strong arms,
how delighted she was
when they couldn't find any shoes that would fit you.
She asked me
how you were sleeping
and I was filled with sorrow to tell her
that you hadn't slept for seven years,
that a shell from an enormous gun
shattered your ribs
and stripped you of your youth.
So I let the sun set
upon your names and dreams,
put to rest the settled dust
you have become.
Between your life, your death, there is
a distance of six children.

•

Taleb Abd al-Aziz was born in 1953 in Basra, a city in southern Iraq full of palm trees, boats, and reed houses on rivers. His poetry is inspired by the city's history, as well as the history of his ancestors and his family. Even the title of "My Brother's War" combines the personal with the public, while the subtle, quiet lines evoke deep sorrow. Though a personal elegy, the poem's central theme echoes the ancient epic of Gilgamesh, the brother who has been killed reminding us of Gilgamesh's close friend Enkidu who was a hero but was killed by an illness inflicted by the gods. Al-Aziz's older brother was killed in 1988 in the Iran-Iraq War; he was only a few meters away from al-Aziz while they were both fighting in the First Battle of al-Faw. "Is it because death mistook me?" al-Aziz asks in another poem. "Perhaps we just exchanged roles in death's story," he told me. "I couldn't take his corpse away until a week later. He was felled in a minefield. While worms crawled out of his body, I carried him to the center of the city where they were collecting the dead. I became responsible for supporting his wife and raising his six children, though I had my own family to take care of. My mother abandoned her bed and slept on a palm mat on the floor. How could she sleep on cotton, she said, when her son sleeps in dirt?"

Al-Aziz works as a journalist and writes a weekly column for *Al-Mada* magazine. His father was a farmer, and al-Aziz still lives in the house of his birth. "There are places around our orchard," he told me, "where I can still see my brother climbing a tree, or bathing. He was strong, and so tall that they didn't have boots of his size in the military." Like his brother and most Iraqi men of that generation, al-Aziz was involuntarily drafted in the war. In battlefields from Kurdistan in the north to al-Faw in the south, he witnessed the death of many of his relatives and friends. "My Brother's War" was written in 1993, on the fifth anniversary of his brother's death. He said, "I wrote the poem in fifteen minutes but with burning tears." Al-Aziz's poetry books include *Tariikh al-Asaa* (The History of Sorrow, 1994) and *Qabla Kharab al-Basra* (Before Basra's Ruin, 2012).

13.

HIS LIFE

RA'AD ABDUL QADIR
Translated from the Arabic by Dunya Mikhail

At the moment
of the bridge
of crossing
of the shadow
of the step
of the rhythm
of the echo
of the trace of life.
At the moment
of sleep on the other shore
I am the man at the moment of crossing to the shore of sleep
I am the woman not reached by the man at the crossing
I am the sleep
I am the sleep on the other shore
I am the echo
the trace
the shadow
the crossing
the bridge
at the moment of
my life.

•

What I love about the poetry of Ra'ad Abdul Qadir (1953–2003) are the small details that become reference points to essential truths, as if they are atoms quietly and dynamically moving together in a simple yet profound meaning. The landscape of his poetry is fertile, so as soon as Qadir skillfully sows a poetic seed, many questions emerge. Play is important in his poetry, but what's particularly special about the game is that you can reassemble the parts differently every time, thus discovering new things by chance.

Qadir died from a heart attack when he was fifty—the windows of his home were thrown open at the moment of his death. "Ra'ad didn't like to write on a table. He would write in bed," his wife, Ilham, said to her guests after the funeral. She gave some of his friends a stack of his papers and notebooks in which they found eleven unpublished poetry collections. During his lifetime, he'd published only half of what he had written. "His Life" is part of a longer sequence of poems called "Letters to the Other Shore." Qadir's books include *Maraya al-As'ila* (Mirrors of Questions, 1979), *Jawai'iz al-Sana al-Kabisa* (Prizes of the Leap Year, 1995), *Opera al-amira al-da'ia'* (Opera of the Lost Princess, 2000), and *Saqr fawqa ra'sihi shams: a'sr al-tasliya* (Eagle with Sun Overhead: The Age of Entertainment, 2006). He earned a doctorate in Islamic history from the University of Baghdad and worked as the managing editor of the literary magazine *Al-Aqlam*.

14.

THE GUARD

ABDULZAHRA ZEKI

Translated from the Arabic by Khaloud al-Muttalibi

The guard behind me
is also beside me and in front of me.
The guard who accompanies me
sometimes precedes me
and other times lingers
unseen, my shadow.
The guard who was born with me
through my long sleep was awake
for every second.
I drank from his glass.
He ate from my plate.
He was there between myself and a road
I never walked.
He was there between my tongue and words
I never spoke.
During the war, he was there between my finger
and the trigger of the gun.
The guard back then
didn't care about the world,
still young, he is
obsessed with me
wary of me
as he watches
I guard him, afraid
he might grow old.

•

Abdulzahra Zeki was born in 1955 in Amara in southern Iraq, and currently works as a cultural adviser for the Department of Cultural Affairs in Baghdad. "The Guard" is from his fifth poetry collection, *Silent Tape: Words About Cars, Bullets, and Blood*, published in 2011. The book is composed of short documentary poems about the U.S. occupation of Iraq that began in 2003. Unlike his earlier, more geographically expansive poems, this collection conveys a suffocating sense of urgency as it chronicles daily events in Baghdad. The guard in his poem wants to protect and to be protected, while life is but a deferment of death. "I walk from home to work not knowing in what moment the explosion will happen," Zeki once said to me. One day he left his office for lunch with two colleagues, and while eating at a restaurant they heard a loud explosion. It turned out that a bomb had fallen on their office building. He said, "I later saw that the bomb had actually penetrated the wall where I used to sit in my office, and pieces of it were all over the floor." In those daily moments of facing death and escaping it, Zeki imagines a guard that accompanies him at all times and then he expresses fear that this guard, like everybody else, would get old. The concern is doubled: fear for one's own age (if the guard is his own self) and fear for one's life with lack of protection (if the guard is another self and would eventually die after getting too old). Zeki explains, however, that the guard symbolizes his consciousness that protects him from other forms of death. The guard "was awake" and that perhaps was what saved the poet.

15.

LIKE HYPATIA IN ANCIENT TIMES

SIHAM JABBAR

Translated from the Arabic by Soheil Najm

My hands are your hands
and your mouth my mouth.
You are part of the darkness
inside me, the darkness
of a lonely woman's throne.

Your hands are not my hands
nor your mouth my mouth.
You are not the confused eyes in the darkness
nor are you the darkness.
There is no throne for a lonely woman.

Like Hypatia in ancient times
they skinned me as I
calculated the mathematical
relationship between time
and our aging bodies.
As I grafted new skin onto me
I squeezed the witness from their sight
and found they had changed
though I stayed the same.

I bathed in ancient philosophies
beside beheaded sculptures;
I besieged the murderers
at the wall.
Perhaps they are barbarians
or wandering Bedouins.
The gods decreed
a labyrinth to grow from our fingers
as each hand is lost
and each love wilderness.
What could the beasts see
in my blood?
A hand will close around my heart
and squeeze the passion from it.
They will seal me in a coffin
that becomes a bomb
death a new explosion
that splatters the labyrinth with blood.

You are sentenced to many decades
of my repeated sufferings.
Thirty have passed
not quite forty
though the century has just begun.
Survival, it is said, is for the fittest
though I'm far from the fittest.
They distribute my blood.
My arteries are for a wise man's death
my brain is food for Satan.
Still they get drunk
yet you are still heedless.
Can you inject my blood with silence

and my love with patience.
Why children?
Stop.
As the decades pass
more skin is peeled off.
The mathematical relationship
won't work unless students
can preserve their wisdom in vials.

How full did the thornbush bloom
with you in the vial
fully flowering?
Blood drips out
instead of a sweet fragrance.
How many springs ended for a country to begin?
Dancing in the cradle, never sleeping.
Umbilical cord cut but the baby was never born.

Move on, my country
beyond your land
your sky
your oil
and my dress.
Leave and rise elsewhere
as if you were a runaway people
as if I gave birth to you, then forgot about you
as if you were an undutiful son,
deprived of my inheritance.
I am just a lonely woman
and you are only ... a traitor.

•

Siham Jabbar was born in Baghdad in 1963, and now lives in Sweden where she teaches Arabic for a living. She wrote "Like Hypatia in Ancient Times" in 2005 when the war in Iraq reached a peak with insurgencies, kidnappings, suicide bombings, and sectarian violence. On her way home from the University of Baghdad where she taught Arabic literature, Jabbar was injured by a stray bullet. "I had just finished teaching a class about theories of criticism," Jabbar told me. Hypatia was a Platonic philosopher and mathematician who lived in Alexandria, Egypt, around the fourth century. She was beheaded and skinned because of her liberal thinking. Like Hypatia, Jabbar paid a price for being in the wrong place at the wrong time. The Egyptian scholar and philosopher Hypatia had many students, but she was accused of extremism and killed because of her teachings, which were too radical for her times. Jabbar was more fortunate in that she survived, though she writes in her poem: "Survival, it is said, is for the fittest / though I'm far from the fittest." The internal tension of the poem revolves around citizen and country, which she directly addresses at the end: "as if I gave birth to you, then forgot about you." This is a popular saying among Iraqis, used to complain about someone who is too attached to the point of becoming a burden, though in her poem Jabbar uses it to express both attachment to and detachment from her country.

ACKNOWLEDGMENTS

My thanks to Ilya Kaminsky for his invitation to edit this *Poets in the World* series pamphlet of fifteen Iraqi poets as part of the Poetry Foundation's *Poetics of Six Continents* program, which began as a three-month correspondence with the poet Katie Ford. Her questions about Iraq's poetic traditions opened my eyes to issues I had never even thought about before. As part of this program, Ford wrote an important essay about the poetics of Iraq that was too long to include in this publication.

I am deeply grateful to Jeffrey Yang for his tremendous editorial work and patience, and to Barbara Epler, who is among the few publishers in the U.S. dedicated to international literature.

Lastly, I would also like to thank all the poets and translators for their contribution.

Fifteen Iraqi Poets is part of a collaboration with the *Poets in the World* series created by the Poetry Foundation's Harriet Monroe Poetry Institute. The *Poets in the World* series supports research and publication of poetry and poetics from around the world and highlights the importance of creating a space for poetry in local communities.

The Harriet Monroe Poetry Institute is an independent forum created by the Poetry Foundation to provide a space in which fresh thinking about poetry, in both its intellectual and practical needs, can flourish free of allegiances other than to the best ideas. The Institute convenes leading poets, scholars, publishers, educators, and other thinkers from inside and outside the poetry world to address issues of importance to the art form of poetry and to identify and champion solutions for the benefit of the art. For more information, please visit www.poetryfoundation.org / institute.

The Poetry Foundation, publisher of *Poetry* magazine, is an independent literary organization committed to a vigorous presence for poetry in our culture. It exists to discover and celebrate the best poetry and to place it before the largest possible audience. The Poetry Foundation seeks to be a leader in shaping a receptive climate for poetry by developing new audiences, creating new avenues for delivery, and encouraging new kinds of poetry through innovative partnerships, prizes, and programs. For more information, please visit www.poetryfoundation.org.

HARRIET MONROE POETRY INSTITUTE
POETS IN THE WORLD SERIES

Publications
Ilya Kaminsky, 2011–2013, HMPI director
Poets in the World series editor

Another English: Anglophone Poems from Around the World, edited by Catherine Barnett and Tiphanie Yanique (Tupelo Press)

Elsewhere, edited by Eliot Weinberger (Open Letter Books)

Fifteen Iraqi Poets, edited by Dunya Mikhail (New Directions Publishing)

"Landays: Poetry of Afghan Women" edited by Eliza Griswold (*Poetry* magazine, June 2013)

New Cathay: Contemporary Chinese Poetry, edited by Ming Di (Tupelo Press)

Open the Door: How to Excite Young People about Poetry, edited by Dorothea Lasky, Dominic Luxford, and Jesse Nathan (McSweeney's)

Pinholes in the Night: Essential Poems from Latin America, edited by Raúl Zurita and Forrest Gander (Copper Canyon Press)

Seven New Generation African Poets, edited by Kwame Dawes and Chris Abani (Slapering Hol Press)

Something Indecent: Poems Recommended by Eastern European Poets, edited by Valzhyna Mort (Red Hen Press)

The Star by My Head: Poets from Sweden, coedited and translated by Malena Mörling and Jonas Ellerström (Milkweed Editions)

The Strangest of Theatres: Poets Writing Across Borders, edited by Jared Hawkley, Susan Rich, and Brian Turner (McSweeney's)

Katharine Coles, HMPI inaugural director

Blueprints: Bringing Poetry into Communities, edited by Katharine Coles (University of Utah Press)

Code of Best Practices in Fair Use for Poetry, created with American University's Center for Social Media and Washington College of Law

Poetry and New Media: A Users' Guide, report of the Poetry and New Media Working Group (Harriet Monroe Poetry Institute)